Same Difference

Same Difference

Ben Wilkinson

Seren is the book imprint of
Poetry Wales Press Ltd.
Suite 6, 4 Derwen Road, Bridgend, Wales, CF31 1LH
www.serenbooks.com
facebook.com/SerenBooks
twitter@SerenBooks

ISBN: 9781781726488
Ebook: 9781781726501

A CIP record for this title is available from the British Library.

The publisher acknowledges the financial assistance of the Books Council of Wales.

Cover painting: 'Love and Grief' by John Hoyland (2006; acrylic on cotton duck;
60 × 50 inches). © Estate of John Hoyland. All rights reserved, DACS 2022

Printed in Bembo by Severn, Gloucester.

Contents

My 'I' has gone farther and farther away from me. Today it is my farthest 'you'.

Antonio Porchia, *Voices*

I do not know which of us has written this page.

Jorge Luis Borges
'Borges and I', *Labyrinths*

Poetry

Let's say the game is as good as up. Scrawled
more of these than I care to remember?
Certainly to talk about. I'll write
another soon enough, even though
the word is done at least you know
in the hands of chumps like us who've said
what's what whoever we are but look
in here and see whatever you want.
Who's speaking this and who's listening
I pretend I couldn't give a fuck
but we both know better, don't we.
Dear reader, just know I'm somewhere here
and feel the shit that drags for all of us.
Everyone and no one. Perhaps that's enough.

Weirdos

A burp of laughter in the boardroom
or sombre at a birthday party,
we spy each other quick as sweat.

Fitful sleep in the passenger seat?
Check. Introspective in rain like you
forgot your own name? You bet.

Here's a gin in a whisky tumbler
to us, who sit in the theatre's
singular dark to watch the full

credits run and beyond; who hear
the fox's cry in the night and think
it some portent; who seriously

work away at poems, as if poems
might shape strangeness into charm,
or box the latest *faux pas* we've

played over and over and over
in the auditorium of our thoughts
this long deserted night. Day comes

just as surely as we are ourselves,
goggle-eyed and fretful by turns,
weird fish preoccupied with water.

A New City

after Cavafy

So I said to myself: I'll move to a new city,
a new country, some other place
better than this one. Sometimes I think
I can't move for my past around here;
the ghosts file through me in every park,
every bar. It's like the mouldy novel of my life,
and I just keep turning the dog-eared pages.

But I haven't left – and maybe I won't ever,
or can't. This city's like the smell of smoke
deep in an old jacket; disgustingly nostalgic.
You can hope for things elsewhere, but
then you can hope for a different personality.
If I've wasted my life here, I guess I'd waste
it anywhere. So I say to myself, anyway.

What We Were

Here's the time we got lost coming off the mountain,
me in shorts and you in a down jacket.
Here's the time I just started sort of uncontrollably
crying, in bed with you in that old cottage.
And look, the nights we sat up all hours
drinking whisky and playfully arguing
about any book or subject that took our fancy.

Here's us taking a bath together, the lather
in your hair like good ice cream. Here's the memory
of us seeing curlews over the far fields,
like clumsy punctuation or a child's drawing.
I think I've always been deluded and romantic
but I keep too much to myself, except in poems.
Here's us kissing in that tiny kitchen.

Here's us in Spain, eating olives in a power cut.
Here's the day we cycled miles on end just to drink
the famous beer in the town where they brew it.
Here's the year we knew bliss
as it poured from a tap we'd just leave running.
Here's the last photo of us. No, wait,
here's another one. Though I don't remember that day.

Mind the Gap

Mind your head on the way in. Mind who you
tell. Mind your language. Mindless violence.
Do you mind? Mind your own business.
Mind is where the heart is. Mind what you say.
Growth mindset. Mind-body dualism. Mind
the kids on a Saturday morning. Let's mind map.

Mind over matter. Mind my grief, would you?
Mind of a criminal. I honestly don't mind.
Dirty mind. Mind the gum stuck to your shoe.
I mind, therefore I am. Mind your Ps and Qs.
Mind you. Mind, brain and personal identity.
Multiple minds theory. Mind as faithful servant;

mind as terrible master. Mind that dog mess.
Mind of his own. Mind sex. Test your mind. Alas,
poor mind. It's make-your-mind-up time.
Two minds are better than one. Too many minds
spoil the thought. Sweet mind o' mine. Mind?
I couldn't care less. The mind of the mob

is slow and feeble. Great minds think alike.
Change your mind. Of one mind. No one
really minds. Minder. This little mind of mine.
You are always on my mind. Mind yourself.
Mind for children. Mind control. Mind your
feet, please, as the trolley passes through.

The Bull

it came to my granddad   like a snorting bull
everyone could see it   he couldn't
horns shaking at the dinner table   crockery
against the wall   my mum   staring
in disbelief   an upended chair   that hot
hot presence   held like the words
that get said   and can't   be taken back
a wedding   the best man's speech   silence
after the storm   tears through the village
it could have been domestic   cat-like
the way for some it hangs   like a fattening
fruit bat   suckling   no less real for that
but for him   it was   the bull alright
brazen   brutish   the stamping beast
that is   there   and not there
unbiddable   it circled   his one-bed flat
matadors to the last   we all found
the red rag   worn by any   unwitting
caller   and that   as they say   was that

Your anxiety

is the souped-up boy racer revving at the lights
beyond this door. Sure he's brash and insecure, a mess
like us all, but fuck it if anyone's gonna stop him.
Tonight's the night he flies out at the red
as you writhe in bed, every thought a near-miss,
the death-kiss his tyres give as they hiss
through rain the same fear gnawing at your brain
in the wee hours. Your eyes are his head-beams,
wide, unblinking, seeing only what they want to see.
Your breath: the motor pulse of wheel spin on a car park;
your heartbeat: the flick of fag ash from his window.
He is sleeplessness, the same loop of a few blocks
till dark breaks, bleeds to light. And you are
awake, again, waiting for things to come right.

Mam Tor

All winter we ran across the moors,
the doors to the peaks blown open

by blizzards or taken clean off their
hinges, like those ancient houses

on gale-torn summits. Winnats Pass
was closed but we skipped the warning

that day-like-night, parked halfway up
its ice-age helter-skelter, stumbled out.

What were we thinking all that long,
long year, barely seeing what was right

up ahead? At the trig point we swore
we saw a figure, hunched and cursing

in the sleet. We trudged back down
as if it were a coffin path, each of us

counting out our own metred feet.

The Flower Carrier

after the painting by Diego Rivera, 1935

These blooms are for the mayor's daughter,
a wedding on which a town pins its hopes.
Soon they'll set long tables creaking,

throng streets in hanging baskets,
thread buttonholes of businessmen,
diplomats. If I were a cynic I'd call them

fig leaves; decoration to perfume
the stench of politics and little else.
But their weight on my back

is the weight of love itself, bright
yet strangely heavy; the faith we all carry
in our tired old hearts. I'll arrive

in town, hat tipped against the sun,
pocket my fee, whistle and be gone,
knowing this beautiful lie is my art alone.

Rabbit Stew

You've seen the stills from the slaughterhouse,
chickens clucking in warehoused stink;
seen carcasses hacked into choice cuts,
the death we make to fill the plate.

But isn't life always give and take?
There's misery in all we make –
fuel your car for another far-flung war;
buy T-shirts stitched in sweating, lonely hours.

The taste is one our ancestors knew
would see them through the ice-bound days,
a spark of flame to part flesh, the ink-dark
blood. To kill and eat as we hate and love

is to know the cost is forever too much;
whatever brief light we might cup
interrupts a timeless dark. As meliorists
we chew the cud, but return to life

none the wiser for wisdom, tugged
along by hunger, the moment's rank want.
Come. I know a farmer who strings rabbits
gassed from warrens that riddle his plot;

he'll let them go for nothing in the pub.
As a boy I was taught to skin and slice
with a tenderness you couldn't call love;
to leave bubbling the primeval swamp

laced, somehow, with heavenly aroma.
We'll serve it up with hunks of bread,
talk politics and passion till we're tired,
but know the age it took to nurture

gave us scope for poems, stories, songs.
Far into the night the ears prick up, quiver
at the field's edges. Look. You can still
make out the eyes' fierce gleam, stealing

across dawn, as you take the long way home.

October

after Verlaine

Here it comes now – autumn's evening –
the setting sun sparking leaves into life.
Death fills the fields with its single word
like the *thwack* of a kitchen knife.

Nothing comes close to the truest season,
free of summer's callow passions.
Watch it wait with its store of darkness,
making sketches of all that might happen.

Of course those nutters and pushovers
all go for spring and dawn, lovers who
looked better the drunken night before.

Me? I'll take autumn's cruel stare
over summer's pining dove.
Its cold, sharp glance is the real look of love.

What the Doorman Says

with a nod to C.R.

That he could kill for a smoke.
That the punters get older every year.
That really, he hardly ever has to lay a finger.
That even arterial blood washes right out.
That the fella with the dog sat at the furthest end of the bar
    is, all told, a cunt.
That sometimes he dreams of jacking it all in, moving to Cornwall
    to open a fish 'n' chip shop.
That booze, generally speaking, brings out the worst in everyone.
That his wife could be anywhere now.
That he's been dry for five years, since she left, bar the one lapse.
That he's seen it all before.
That you didn't need to worry about a gang of blokes as much as
    a serious hen party rocking up.
That letting punters choose the music from a jukebox with an
    internet connection is a stupid idea.
That I should mind my own business.
That he could kill for a smoke.
That too many kids have knives on them nowadays.
That the punters get older every year.
That you learn a thing or two about life watching a grown man
    fall down on his own vomit.
That he wouldn't let his daughter near this place.
That a good strong cup of tea will do him nicely, ta.
That booze, generally speaking, brings out the worst.

The Young Fools

after Verlaine

We were always first to hit the town back then,
   supping pints and blowing smoke rings.
Those devastating girls in mascara and heels
   left us gawking with their gorgeous dancing.

On nights of enough drink and courage
   we'd step up to offer cocktails, their dresses
fizzing with the mirror ball's shimmer
   in which we might weigh up our chances.

Then the small hours, pairing off to wander –
   each with our girl in the sweet summer air –
as the whispers that set our hearts pounding
   faded, like night with the morning's glare.

The Middle of the Midlands

I was done, and we were too,
        after that long summer the glassy
                scars on your arm reopened
one by one; a party where I stepped

out for air and a smoke to find
        some tool with his tongue
                down your throat. Seeing red
wasn't my style, so you doubled efforts

for the both of us: a stiletto heel
        aimed with a markswoman's eye;
                the full, frothing pint in the face.
I'd've blamed your mum for the spite

and the hate but I saw, even then,
        the same raw hurt on her,
                thought of what the poet said
about handing on misery, the coastal shelf. Autumn

was already in the air as I cycled away
        from your mid-terraced house,
                a new term and exams to come,
though we felt like we were adults.

What a joke. I remember pausing
        in the road at a seagull, of all things,
                staring me down – here, in the middle
of the Midlands – then patting my jean

pockets as if I'd maybe lost something.
                Forget that, I thought, and cycled on.

You Can See How It Was

Home is just odd. Days it sort of waits there,
a cave full of nothing, or stalactites
you negotiate by feel when the light peters
and fades. Foxhole we hate to love, it's like
a cosy lover one week, living underwater

the next. Don't get me wrong: you need one,
and without, by choice or cruelty, we clock
reality, like the woodsman without a gun
facing a grizzly. But look at the place. A mock
museum, curated by its one strange specimen.

Invocation

Here's to hope that, decades on, I still remember it all –
how the rain played a heavy beat on the skylight
the nights I sat reading Derrida then *Not Saussure*,
cigarette smoke drifting from the ashtray on my desk,
Sam and Joe in stitches at the third season of *Scrubs*,
mornings when that brunette undressed before a window
and must've known that half the street might see her,
the day we found POLICE LINE – DO NOT CROSS sealing off
Eastwood Road, uncovering an attic full of marijuana,

and our unruly garden, all weeds, one growing to six feet
in three weeks when we left the place over Easter,
the distant throb of techno filtering through the windows,
our living room's threadbare carpet, textured white walls,
the nightly wailing alarm of some Corsa, Aygo or Golf,
that evening we played *Articulate!* while pissed, Brawley
somehow confusing Charles Dickens with Oliver Twist,
those final months brimming with all this, the milk bottles
sitting on our porch uncollected, full with stagnant water,

my hair curly, wild and unkempt and three times longer
than it ever was or has been since, Roney's bacon baps
twice a week for breakfast, kids on BMXs flying along
the pavements, summer days of rain continually pouring
while the leak from our attic's knackered shower snaked
behind the wallpaper, long Friday nights at the Lescar,
junk mail, misdirected mail and flyers dropping through
the letterbox, jars and tubs of stuff sat in the fridge forever,
eating tinned soup, pasta bake, Marmite on toast, muesli,

the long walk from Brocco Bank up towards Walkley,
early hours' laughter heading home from The Leadmill,
the *Guardian*, ten deck of Marlboros, and pint of milk
from the newsagents, the radio blaring, Rich singing
'Club Tropicana' as he scrambled eggs in our kitchen,
the pollen count through the roof, the lead clean stolen
in the middle of the night from the local church's roof,
and all of us, for the last time, gathered in that front room,
our stuff in boxes, sitting, waiting, with the rain hurling down.

We apologise

that the 18:18 to Cleethorpes has been cancelled due to:

leaves on the line – fuel shortage – intergalactic warfare –
WiFi interference patterns – spilt latte from the buffet cart –
the spontaneous combustion of a staff member –
dark matter – the axis of evil – a carriage coupling issue –
major fault – extreme weather – fluctuating value of the pound –
cognitive dissonance – irretrievable mass data loss –
your mum – the Gulf stream – platform wobbliness –
please listen for further announcements – narcoleptic driver –
insufficient rail capacity – unexpected item in the bagging area –
mechanical anxiety – enfant terrible – musical epidemic –
Schlemmel's disease – the last scintilla of doubt –
time's arrow – widespread ennui – insert/delete as appropriate –

Ocean

Again they gather, wide-eyed and at the same time
each day. Hairless creatures, tap-tapping at the glass.

They see me, I guess, as some sideshow of the past –
monster of the deep, trapped and viewable for a fee.

The smaller types clamour, silently chatter, jump
up and down as I glide in, but still to a hush

when I centre my wheelhub stare into their souls.
Others slouch, prod at screens in tentacled grip

or, loosening the tie round their necks, shuffle off
cradling a slip of black gemstone to bowed heads.

The old I like best. When their ancient eyes meet mine,
mournful, I'm sure they know what it is to lose

an ocean, that endlessness, stretched out before you.

Coach

Sometimes I think I've hovered
here all my life, stopwatch in hand,

rasping the splits of another set
of reps. From sweat-soaked

summers of morning track meets
to the stadium glare of autumn's

floodlights, I've devised and
delivered variations on a theme:

pain. It's what brings them all,
whether Olympic hopefuls or

driven amateurs; those in search
of redemption, or the switch

to turn it off. What I give them
is the space to make it good –

a perfect loop of lined cinder, honest
and flat; the sense that it matters

if it matters to them enough.
Some just want encouragement;

others, tough love. I don't need
the backstory. There are many

reasons to test the limits
of the human heart,

and this business of ours
as good as any. On your marks.

The Champion

Because what I love best is the sweat,
swift force of will supplanting strength,
forehand cross-court with enough spin
to take your head off. Watch the racket
warp above his glare, fighter pilot's
propeller throttling on the ascent,
dent after dent in his opponent's
confidence, winners he's no right to hit.

Who wouldn't want to watch that, grit
and graft above effortless grace?
Beauty's for novices; success a story
of setback, repetition. Persistence
makes the moment you'll watch again
and again, a burst of chalk or clay
as time and space bend to make way.

Church of the Sunday Long Run

Wake before dawn. Don shorts
and harrier tee, tie laces
silently. Percolate coffee, careful
to sip as it cools and you turn
your thoughts to the road ahead.

The warmup mile you must respect:
pay attention to breath,
your pulse a compass needle,
at first wavering, then dead set.
Nod to those fellow devotees

you meet at intervals as your
GPS watch counts the miles.
Before you know it, you are at
the zen heart, truly midrun
in woods you knew as a child.

Never shirk from the final hill,
light pulsing through clouds.
Birdsong will cheer you home,
a city waking as sweat anoints
your brow. You see it now.

Meaning

The child doesn't care why they run. Happy with sunlight
on her freckled back she dips fingers into long rushes,

reaches an imagined finish line in record time, no
starter's gun to fire a stride that speaks happiness,

pure movement, the bold act itself. When she stops,
breathless, hot hands holding scuffed knees, you

pause too; almost spot yourself. What happened
to that wild soul who once leapt stiles into owled fields,

the hour before dark? Her heart is this opened grip,
clasped and then released. This moment. Take it.

The Nightingale

after Verlaine

The two of us lolling in the park
with silence sweeping the green,
as a summer day fizzles out
in the static, darkening leaves.

Once, love came easily enough –
the scent of those tall lime trees
setting our eager hearts off
like a jackpot's flood of pennies.

Instead, we close our eyes now,
shut into private half-dreams,
and the gap between us
opens up, sudden and unseen.

Love, let's be convinced at last
we trust what the other means.
Life shuttles by way too fast
for these doubtful little games.

Then, when evening comes down,
throwing its shadows across us,
we'll hear the nightingale singing,
whose song is one of clearness.

1963

Everyone knows that moment,
its twisted, time-lapsed dream logic,

but to feel its weight each day
the way I held his lifeless body

as the car screamed away
is more than anyone should bear.

All the clichés are true –
he was my hero, a man taken

in his prime; the good always
die young while the crooks

get re-elected for a second term.
I don't want pity. I know to some

I'm just the winsome face, the wife
who spruced up the White House;

the truth is too complicated
to interest most, so let history

take its course. Imagine seeing
what happened to my man

happen to yours. You can't.
The years speed by like gunshot

echoes out, horror followed
by the inevitable quietude;

the numbness of what, finally,
we remember to forget.

Portrait of the Artist Asleep

after Verlaine

She looks for all the world like some deadbeat angel,
foetal but hopeful, an inch of light haloing

her temple. She's restless, sure, half mumbling
to herself as the door rocks gently in its frame,

stirred by a breeze the way her waking thoughts
follow whatever her eyes light on, even you.

Truth is, she'll be up and gone before you know,
back among the world and brilliant with it,

and you, friend, won't even make a painting
or poem, whichever she turns her hand to next.

You're no more her muse than the lamp distilled
in the mirror she'll fix her face in before she leaves.

Once

after Verlaine

Memories, memories... what do you want of me?
The year's good as gone and summer is dead.
A sun that's its own perfect facsimile
glints through the trees that drift up ahead.

Here I go again, dawdling in this daydream,
thoughts gone haywire in a whistling gale.
Ghostly, her glossy eyes turn to fix me –
How long is it since we were last here then?

Who knows, but her voice is like an angel's;
her touch, those fireflies swarming at dusk.
I know the risks in blundering back here,

revelling in that glorious, summer-day fuck.
Take these day-glo flowers, their perfect scent;
her fulsome kiss. It came and it went.

Grey Disgust

is unexpected dogshit speckling the soles of your shoes.
It is stepping into a lift still rich with the grim fart of the
previous occupant. It is the bloated bread, bulbous at
the back of the bin; the bacon curled, anaemic, in the
fridge's irritated bowels. It is this businessman, trawling
the quayside looking for his soul on a rank Monday
night; it is the type of public toilet you enter and are
immediately afraid to leave, lest the next person thinks
you did the god-knows-what-the-fuck-went-on-in-here
on entry. It is that look she gave you, just the once. It is
here, there and everywhere and it is here to stay; it is
the underbelly of each day which waits like teeming
woodlice, say, crawling under that rock, or the nest of
hair and product you don't have the stomach to hook
from the shower plughole, not yet. It is a tiny god,
miserable and balding, picking absent-mindedly at his
belly-button fluff.

after Mary Ruefle

Fuzz

'04, sweat slinking up the walls,
this dive our holy temple to
sing and move. Cheap snakebite
and black sets the groove;

we spark up cigs like every other
indier-than-thou here strutting
to The Strokes, Arcade Fire, Muse.
The bass thumps through the floor

and our pupils fucking bloom;
two-day-old shoes flecked with
the sludge that clings, cakes.
In the loos, a locked cubicle

emits groans; the hand-drier moans
as a pint's spilled on some random
with Ziggy Stardust make-up. But
now's the chorus to this month's

definitive tune, all of us briefly
gorgeous in its seismic wake,
till the lights go up and we make
for the exits. At the taxi rank

we shiver in early morning's rain,
skin up under coats and hoods;
each orange light a blessing
before the sunrise's bleary curse.

Cage

Truth is, I lost my front teeth in '96 –
third round, sweat clinging to the walls,
pound-pound of a busted car alarm

in my skull. This business ain't flower
arranging. You go *mano a mano*, the animal
look in the eyes, tribal thump of the mob;

silence when the first blood draws.
But there's beauty in it, too: fear teaches
anyone about themselves. One minute

you're cock of the walk, crowing over
the fallen, next you're the one hitting
the deck, hearing the chorus

of a thousand devils. I know your type,
thinking every skinhead is some
chest-beater for the far right. Right?

There's tenderness to this; a kind of love
in hauling your broken brother up, sensing
the fine balance our lives hang in,

knowing the fight can never be won.

Fame

Buried in the four-storeys

       of market-playing geniuses

or more often than not

       in the mansions of the famous,

the panic room sits tight

       till shadows grace the cameras.

Then its door's swung shut,

       with no way in and the fear

of climbing out; the heist

       televised on its grainy monitor

as the landline clicks dead

       and the lights begin to flicker.

Joie de Vivre

after Verlaine

Now you suckers and saps might fall for nature
but that confidence trickster doesn't fool me.
All those touched-up pastorals of half-assed
emotion are the last thing I want to see.

Art's a total joke, and we're no better –
I laugh at verse, the churches' fawning spires,
and worse, Canary Wharf's effervescence,
that Midas touch turning the whole lot to shit.

Assholes and good guys are one of a kind.
I've left behind faith, daydreams, and as for
love – *please*. Let's wave all that goodbye.

Like a useless toy boat that's miles offshore –
too tired to go on, but who can't pack it in –
I'll wait on the shipwreck still gunning for me.

Rich

I get that they're not all called Tarquin
and Allegra, lording over the grounds

of the manor as the servants curtesy
and sweat. Or out in the meadows

gunning pheasants, dawbing their young
fox-red while slathering dogs grunt

and bay. Money spoils whether it falls
in the lap or accrues in the hands:

from this silver spoon to that shimmer
of Rolls Royce, purring behind twenty

-foot gates. Show me someone rolling in it
and I'll show you their misspent contempt;

myth of the self-made that keeps us plebs
in our place. Think Jacob Rees-Mogg;

think *Scarface*. Think Harry Enfield's
'Loadsamoney' before the garish glare

of Thatcher's England, laughter track
with a vengeance. Think winner

takes it all in a fixed game with loaded
dice, a marked deck, you name it. Pick

a card. Any card. It makes no difference.

Guacamole

Though he later denied it, Labour politician Peter Mandelson reportedly once mistook a Hartlepool fish and chip shop's mushy peas for the considerably more middle-class avocado dip.

— *The Telegraph*, May 2017

Like the posh lad who swanned up
to the counter of a fish 'n' chip shop
asking for a battered haddock and
some of that delicious-looking guacamole
there are brilliant poems destined
to be lost on each and every one of us.

This one, say, might light the fag tip
of an epic experience that,
passed to the ex-smoker, lingers
like a memory you can't forget.
It's no more than an inconvenience
to the affected cough, sat at the table across.

Or else it will gallop off, a riderless horse,
ridiculous or frightening in its charge
or both at once, or neither. Whatever.
To be fair, if you mistake mushy peas
for guacamole, you can probably fuck off.

Try living in a house

with rats in the walls. Try not listening
for the scuttle past the headboard.

Try waking in the night at a photo frame
crashing to the floor. Try sleep where

the oil-black form slinks, hisses and dives
into darkening thoughts. Try attic traps,

poison, foam and wire wool packed
into every crevice. Try forgetting.

Try watching, waiting. Try the rustle
of gnawing, decay that crackles

under everything. Try sticking from
the shadows; try what you must.

Try knowing that when they're gone,
they're not. Try this as the story of us.

Lament

after Verlaine

Here now, it's hard to believe this place –
yellowed wallpaper, towels hung over
every decent beer except the guest –
is where we first met and that blur

of brilliance – a world from this pint
and the torn baize of a duff pool table –
meant the next week, the next fortnight,
were the closest things ever get to simple.

So if this is how I know us, want us –
two who clicked on an understanding
of close as close to sparseness, bluntness –
then that's why, aware or drifting,

I've come to sit in this selfsame chair,
selfsame spot, listening to the traffic
which you must be a part of, somewhere,
pitched as it is between frantic and Orphic

while one by one the pigeons flutter off,
draining the glass and closing my book
as the lights click on, someone coughs,
and the place is good as lost, however I look.

Ben, we care

*about you and the memories you share here. We thought
you'd like to look back on this post from six years ago*
mainly because it features a beloved pet you were
estranged from after a hardly acrimonious but
nonetheless wholly unpleasant breakup, and this photo
including former lover, blissfully oblivious to the
future, wearing an oversized jumper you'll recognise
through groggy nostalgia as one of your own, is more
troubling for also preserving the unwavering love that
only a faithful dog – 'those poor creatures we have
gifted a soul for which there is no heaven' – can
communicate with an exactitude (even in this scene,
captured by iPhone and inept photographer) to leave
you crying, suddenly and weirdly crying in the long
queue at the supermarket, wondering why you ever
imagined it a good idea to catalogue your life in a
database which, through vain algorithms, might choose
to spring consequence on you at any given moment.
*We hope you enjoy looking back at your memories on
Facebook, from the most recent, to those from long ago.*

Patient

What I need to tell you is this:

that the day the doctors told me
I felt like I was stood on the precipice,
the wind howling in my hair,

tearing at my tattered winter coat,
snow drifts chattering to an avalanche
and not a soul around. Now

I'm the diver wavering on the edge
of the board: whole hours can pass
with nothing but the thought,

quivering on the lip. If I can execute
the perfect jump, a trained Olympic youth,
I can pass through to the other side

alive, with flawless shimmering technique.
But I am afraid, unsure, out of practise,
and hope waits like a lifeguard, half-asleep

in his chair. There is no-one else here,
and the water grows cold, distant,
unforgiving.

I Dream I'm the Death of Jeff Buckley

You know the folklore –
      how I assumed the force and shift
         of the river's waters, carried

         the melancholy song of one
            already lost to the world,
               carried along and under.

            A wonder, his music was whatever
        whispered through the grassy
banks that day, bittersweet

glister of love and memory.
        But we were one by then –
           impossible to tell form from flow,

           matter from depths, as the song
              becomes the singer, the singer
                 lost in song. We are gone,

              and all that remains
          of that dream-dredged
        moment is flotsam:

        the held note, an empty bottle,
          this lump in the throat
             as the record gives grace.

The Time Machine

Back to the edge of the city dump
it stands, conspicuous, as if a jump
through decades had brought it here
by accident: some elsewhere
in which a bloke in dark overcoat
and bowler watches it blur and float
into nothingness, the ciggie dropped
from his mouth. This poppy-red box
has you stunned and reeling too:
back to a time when the darkness grew
far around its little torch of light
while you whispered goodnight
to her faded name across the miles,
or saw another broken and defiled
by some drunken, bloodied fist;
splintered glass with a violent kiss.
It hits you hard when you step inside:
the faint, fusty smell a joyride
gone wrong; the handset left hung
by its own noose; the swansong
of those incessant, rising notes.
You slip a coin down its throat
but it spits it back out.
Stood in its tiny realm of doubt
there is nothing left to say or do,
the world beyond its windows
short-changing, forgetful and cruel;
but then the mobile's gabble
starts and you wake up, the door
swung to as it fades out of focus.

Church Going

It's boarded shut but with a broken lock,
this door you push open onto dusk –
smashed bottles, random junk, the chalk
graffiti that bids you *Fuck Off.* Dust
spirals up, clinging to the spectres
in the windows. Some bird flaps about,
crowing and shitting from the rafters.
A gale blows outside, a hymn to doubt.

When churches fall completely out of use,
what shall we turn them into ... Not much.
This one's earmarked for apartments,
yet for years has seen nothing but loose
plaster crumble with the rot. Darkness.
A piano's dead keys, cold to your touch.

Last Hope

after Verlaine

Bustled about in this sputtering breeze
the graveyard's oak seems wild and free,
as if it weren't crowded with heavy
stones or the millpond's dying gleam.

Still, it offers up that faithful song
of a blackbird perched in the wings.
Again it gives a bittersweet tune
to the highway's roar of engines.

I could almost see you as that bird,
myself as the lumbering tree.
Or almost dream our love again –

some dressed-up, perfect memory.
Instead, of course, stuff falls apart…
But what to say? Hell – where to *start*?

Frame

Our life is not our life, merely the story we have told ourselves.
— Julian Barnes, *The Sense of an Ending*

I've been trying to write this one for years:
it ends with me leaving a framed print

of the two of us held above Grasmere
by the bins out back of the crumbling flat

I rented, after we went south. A summer
we catalogued the peaks and lakes

with hikes we'd swear were the happiest
of our lives, all harm on ice and us

in our element. Scratch that. Let's jump
back another five years, a host of near

misses like the millions of moments
that might but don't happen every day:

freak weather, train delays, divine will,
you name it; a night we shared a friend's

floor after a gig and Laphroaig,
or single beds in the same room

as that portrait of Ted Hughes
— remember? — looking soberly awkward

with Auden & co. I think we knew
already then, don't you. Here's us

three years later, drinking in the Bull,
night pressing its face to the window

as that sudden intensity which comes
around the third beer kicks in,

our eyes locked with effortless talk –
a sure sign of trouble. Just memory

and its neat shot of treachery;
the chaser you'll knock back anyway.

Was there ever really a prelude –
awkward, unsure – to afternoons spent

confiding about everything, as if we'd
stumbled on some smuggler's cove,

hidden from the thunder of the sea?
We'd visit the place week after week,

introduce the language of our bodies,
acting like tomorrow we'd drown

or the whole secret come crashing down.
It sort of did. But who can stay apart

when there's gravity to contend with,
like the moon's sorry listing for the lip

of an ocean? We were fools rowing
out and out, never thinking our boat

was splintering, though anyone can
look back and rewrite themselves. Once,

when I was alone and halfway drunk,
I let the ghosts of what we were

file through me, settle under my skin.
I thought of you when we met again

at that party, perched smoking on a
fire escape, and well within your rights

to shove me off. A few weeks later
we were deeper than ever: time

would slow almost to a stop, waiting
on the tiny thrill of the phone screen

lighting up, or that gentle knock.
We fled those days. There's a kind

of want that's like some fairy-tale well,
and what we bring up in our little pail

seems so fresh and true and slakes
our thirst like something else, we've

half a mind to jump down into it.
And then we do. The memory of us

(this movie frame held forever
mid-afternoon, the light almost unreal,

a winter sun blotted by snowstorms)
won't tally with the end, those days

run aground into clumsy attempts
at something sailing towards friendship.

It ended with me leaving a framed print.
I've been trying to write this one for years.

This Year

If we could gift each other moments
I'd wrap up that bauble sun we felt
warm our backs to the tip of Mam Tor.

I'd box the two hours spent tracing
the tinselled reservoir, no two miles
the same as we ran and ran, trails

deserted, no sound but our own
good hearts and honest footfall. I'd
ribbon that first jog up Ringinglow,

this city held as if the snow globe
we'd shake. And I'd nestle under
the tree those loops of a floodlit track,

a reminder that what's done is done,
and of dark-bright moments still to come.

Two Foxes

It happens when you drink too much in the park
on an afternoon with the girl you just met,
the weather stuck between sunshine and squall.
And no, I don't mean that. Not yet.

More the way our lives have hidden for months
on hold but now, here, you're noticing
yourself, remembering those two foxes
on a midnight run at the dawn of lockdown,

tentatively sussing the streets, the silence,
each other. You chat around the usual stuff
but then it comes: your eyes lock, and this
could be the start of a story without pandemic:

the precise moment you both recognise it,
fox and vixen, mirroring each other's movements.

A Late Aubade

after Verlaine

How long since we last lolled here all morning,
the house quiet and still, snow falling
beyond our bedroom's window and warmth?
Now we've time to uncover each other
after what seems like months apart –
losing ourselves in that same tender art
to open one thought onto another –
even this grim half-light has a charm of sorts.

Times like these grant us leave from the world –
those claims it makes of everyone –
and the constant doing that comes to nothing;
the snow still falls and the streets are frozen.
Instead, let this moment be perfectly held:
return us to something we hadn't thought missing.

Northern Anecdotal

My mum is standing at the door, laughing.
She's seen some sights but this is me,
twelve at most, covered from head-to-toe
in mud from the riverbed. I've jumped

off Weetman's bridge as a dare,
not guessing the shallow waters there
are home to sludge, shit, quicksand clutching
at my feet. Fetched up on the banks

like a flopping perch the fishermen land,
my pals run off to god-knows where, or when.
I've dragged myself home, a crap monster
from a 50s B movie

to this door, my mum, and her laughter.
But I'm remembering it wrong… not laughter
but anger, hot and sudden. And not mum
but dad, stood dark in the doorway, waiting.

And not the time I jumped off the bridge
but the night I first got pissed, necking
White Lightning till I stumbled back sick.
And not me, but whoever I was. Whoever this is.

Afterword: after Verlaine

The nineteenth-century French poet Paul Verlaine isn't exactly held in the highest regard these days. He lived a life torn between extremes – peace and violence, faith and blasphemy, compassion and lecherousness – briefly embracing a bourgeois life before divorcing his wife; spending time in jail for shooting his sometime lover Arthur Rimbaud; making an unconvincing conversion to Catholicism only to utterly renounce it, before being elected by his peers to the prestigious post of 'Prince of Poets' and dying penniless two years later. Throughout his turbulent life he constantly wrote poetry; in many ways, his continued indecisiveness and inner turmoil both defined his poetic and kept the stuff coming. Coupled with a belief that he might make ends meet through book sales, it meant Verlaine published more than he ever should have. Critics are in agreement: you have to rummage to find the good stuff in a somewhat baggy oeuvre.

Yet the poems *after Verlaine* included in this book have stemmed from my belief that there *are* a number of excellent works of his to be uncovered; that his best poems are not those merely suggestive and allusive pieces as some would have it; and that, in its emotionally honest portrayal of the uncertainties, conflicts, and paradoxes of the examined life, his poetry has a lot to offer to modern readers. Belief being the operative word; at this point, I should make a few things clear. Firstly, my grasp of the French language is limited to say the least; secondly, my intention was never to faithfully translate any of Verlaine's poems. As others have effectively argued to the point that said argument has become near-axiomatic, translation allows much of the surface sense of the original poem to survive, but often results in musical adversity in its commitment to preserving the semantic above all else. I first came to Verlaine's poems in the form of solid, wholly trustworthy translations by Martin Sorrell and Norman R. Shapiro, among others. Each time a translated poem struck me as unusual and interesting, it led me to hunt down cribs, as well as to dig up other translations. In this way, I'd begin to get a feel for what I sensed to be the essence and the argument – or the beating heart and the turbulent mind – hidden at the centre of each poem. For me, this was what had survived translation, in spite of sound and sense parting ways: an echo of Verlaine himself, if you like, in his distinctive yet often adaptable poetic style. It was what I wanted to tap into when I came to write.

On one level, the Verlaine poems here are a selfish project. I wanted to try on a voice with which, despite sharing some stylistic and tonal sympathies, I seemed to have little in common. It served as a psychodramatic exercise, a walk in somebody else's shoes. Writing each new poem while drawing on the raw material of Verlaine in translation has led me, in the always dramatised context of the individual poem, to think and say things I'd likely never have dreamed of otherwise. But just as importantly, I hope these poems paint a fresh portrait of Paul Verlaine, however partial and sketchy, that reveals him to be a more surprising, hard-thinking, and even revivifying poet than expected. Beyond his skilled conjuring of delicate and atmospheric allusiveness, at its best, his is also poetry of punchy musicality, philosophical edge, and candidness – both intellectual and emotional – which allows for genuine beauty, sensuality, and sadness. For all the impressionistic qualities of his poems, he is not in the business of showy or withering obfuscation. Perhaps most of all, as a poet of quiet reflection and stillness, and of pure in-between-ness, his is a voice peculiarly well-suited to our fast-paced, garrulous, and disorienting times.

Sheffield, August 2021

Acknowledgements

Thanks are due to the editors of the publications where the following poems have appeared: *Bad Lilies* ('You Can See How It Was', 'Portrait of the Artist Asleep'); *Blackbox Manifold* ('Fame'); *The Bolton Review* ('Ocean'); *The Edinburgh Review* ('A Late Aubade'); *The French Literary Review* ('Last Hope'); *The Friday Poem* ('What the Doorman Says'); *Like the Wind* ('Meaning'); *Magma* ('Try living in a house', 'Northern Anecdotal'); *METER: the runner's review* ('Church of the Sunday Long Run'); *The New Statesman* ('Mam Tor', 'Weirdos'); *New Welsh Review* ('Invocation'); *POEM* ('Once'); *The Poetry Review* ('Poetry', 'Joie de Vivre', 'October'); *The Spectator* ('A New City', 'Your anxiety', 'The Bull', 'Cage', 'Patient'); *Times Literary Supplement* ('What We Were', 'The Young Fools', 'The Nightingale'); *Wild Court* ('The Flower Carrier', 'The Champion').

'The Nightingale' was the *Times Literary Supplement* Poem of the Week, 3 June 2019.

'Two Foxes' was commissioned as part of DINA Sheffield's 'Small Pleasures' lockdown project (2020).

'This Year' was commissioned for inclusion in *Christmas Presents: Ten Poems to Give and Receive* (Candlestick Press, 2020).

I'm grateful to John Challis, James Giddings, and Niall Campbell, all of whom kindly read different versions of this collection, offering wise critical feedback.

Thanks, as always, to Amy Wack, Mick Felton, Sarah Johnson, and all at Seren.

Setting Suns

after Verlaine

This gloomy dusk
poured over streets
is the sorrow
of setting suns.
What sadnesses
delude us with
a softened song
when hearts forget
how suns will set!
Now my dreams sing
with blazing suns
still sending up
a ghostly world,
sparked and swirled
into ashes.
Such setting suns.